STUDIES IN ENGL

Ge

Da

Already published in the s

Already published in the series (*continued*):

SHAKESPEARE: HAMLET

by

KENNETH MUIR

Emeritus Professor of English Literature
University of Liverpool

EDWARD ARNOLD

© KENNETH MUIR 1963

First published 1963 by
Edward Arnold (Publishers) Ltd
41 Bedford Square, London WC1B 3DQ

Reprinted 1964, 1967, 1969, 1971, 1973, 1975, 1978,
1980, 1983, 1984, 1986

ISBN 0 7131 5077 6

To Arthur H. Fedel
and other Pittsburgh friends

Printed and bound in Great Britain at
The Camelot Press Ltd, Southampton

General Preface

The object of this series is to provide studies of individual novels, plays and groups of poems and essays which are known to be widely read by students. The emphasis is on clarification and evaluation; biographical and historical facts, while they may be discussed when they throw light on particular elements in a writer's work, are generally subordinated to critical discussion. What kind of work is this? What exactly goes on here? How good is this work, and why? These are the questions that each writer will try to answer.

It should be emphasized that these studies are written on the assumption that the reader has already read carefully the work discussed. The objective is not to enable students to deliver opinions about works they have not read, nor is it to provide ready-made ideas to be applied to works that have been read. In one sense all critical interpretation can be regarded as foisting opinions on readers, but to accept this is to deny the advantages of any sort of critical discussion directed at students or indeed at anybody else. The aim of these studies is to provide what Coleridge called in another context 'aids to reflection' about the works discussed. The interpretations are offered as suggestive rather than as definitive, in the hope of stimulating the reader into developing further his own insights. This is after all the function of all critical discourse among sensible people.

Because of the interest which this kind of study has aroused, it has been decided to extend it first from merely English literature to include also some selected works of American literature and now further to include selected works in English by Commonwealth writers. The criterion will remain that the book studied is important in itself and is widely read by students.

DAVID DAICHES

Preface

Anyone who has studied the criticism of the past two hundred years must be aware of the impossibility of producing an interpretation of *Hamlet* which will satisfy even a majority of readers; but I myself, as will be apparent, have learned a great deal even from critics with whom I disagree. I have used the text of Peter Alexander's one-volume Shakespeare, but in a few places I have restored readings of the Second Quarto and the First Folio.

KENNETH MUIR

Since the publication of this book ten years ago, I have devoted chapters to *Hamlet* in *Shakespeare's Tragic Sequence* (1972) and *Shakespeare the Professional* (1973). These modify, if only slightly, one or two of the opinions expressed here.

K.M. 1973

Contents

1. Introduction

A version of *Hamlet*, probably not by Shakespeare, existed as early as 1589, when Nashe alluded to it in his Preface to Greene's *Menaphon*. It was mentioned again by Henslowe in 1594, not as a new play, and by Lodge in 1596. The play belonged to the rival company to Shakespeare's in which Edward Alleyn was the chief actor. *Hamlet* was not listed by Meres as one of Shakespeare's works in 1598, but soon afterwards Gabriel Harvey declared that, unlike *Venus and Adonis*, it could please the wiser sort. A piratical text of Shakespeare's play was published in 1603, in an edition known as the First Quarto. The length of this text is about half that of the full version; but as the pirates reproduced some scenes with remarkable accuracy, while serving up a crude paraphrase of others, it has been assumed that the text was not obtained by the use of stenographers in the theatre, but put together by one or more actors who eked out their imperfect memories with echoes of the source play. Some believe, however, that some characteristics of the First Quarto may be due to the fact that it is based on a version written by Shakespeare in 1598-9, which he revised two or three years later.

The authentic text of the play, released for publication by Shakespeare's company after the appearance of the bad quarto, was probably printed from the poet's own manuscript,[1] or a copy of it. This 1604 edition is known as the Second Quarto. During the next nineteen years the play underwent numerous alterations, for a few of which Shakespeare may have been responsible. *Hamlet* is the longest of his plays, and even when one makes allowance for the rapid delivery of the lines by Elizabethan actors, it can hardly have been played uncut in the normal 'two hours' traffic of the stage'. The most serious cut was Hamlet's last soliloquy, 'How all occasions do inform against me!' A large number of verbal alterations were made, some of them unintentional substitutions by the actors, which thus found

Cf. J. D. Wilson, *The Manuscript of Shakespeare's 'Hamlet'* (1934).

their way into the prompt-book, and others deliberate substitutions, when a word used by Shakespeare had begun to seem archaic or difficult. The First Folio edition (1623), printed directly or indirectly from the prompt-book, embodies the changes made in the text during the intervening years; but it is more carefully printed than the Second Quarto, and it enables us to correct misprints and to supply passages which had been omitted by mistake. A modern edition, therefore, although based on Q2, will also make use of F1; and in a few places the editor may find that even Q1 throws some light on the way the play was performed in Shakespeare's day.[1]

The main source of Shakespeare's play was presumably the Ur-*Hamlet*, as it is called, the play written in the 'eighties by Thomas Kyd or by one of his imitators; but, as Shakespeare often consulted several sources, it is quite possible that he knew the versions of the Hamlet story by Saxo Grammaticus and Belleforest. Although we have no certain evidence about the nature of the Ur-*Hamlet*, there are some slight indications which enable us to guess what it was like. First, it is reasonable to assume that some of the differences between Q1 and Q2 were due to the incorporation of incidents from the old play in the piratical text. Secondly, a German play of the early eighteenth century, *Fratricide Punished*, may be a debased version of the Ur-*Hamlet*, taken to Germany by English actors. Thirdly, it may be assumed that in some ways the Ur-*Hamlet* was closer than Shakespeare's play to the version of the story by Belleforest. Lastly, if the Ur-*Hamlet* was written by Kyd (or by one of his imitators), we should expect it to have some resemblance to *The Spanish Tragedy* in which there is a ghost demanding vengeance, a father seeking to avenge the death of his son and driven distracted by his grief, a woman's suicide, and a play performed as part of the revenge plot. *Hamlet* makes use of a similar plot, although the avenger is a son and not a father.

The revenge play was popular on the Elizabethan and Jacobean stage, but the basic formula could be treated in many different ways. The attitude of the dramatists to revenge ranged from utter condemnation to substantial approval, and it was much less rigid than that of preachers and moralists. Some critics have supposed that

[1] e.g. S. D. III.iv.101, '*Enter the ghost in his night gowne*'.

Shakespeare's hands were tied by the nature of the old play, and that its very popularity, of which there is abundant evidence, would have prevented him from deviating too far from the original. But it is surely probable that he had as much freedom as Sophocles or Euripides had in treating themes already used by Aeschylus. Even when he made use of the incidents of the 'Kyd' play, he could make them mean something totally different by greater subtlety in characterisation.

*   *   *

There was no mystery about *Hamlet* during the first century and a half after it was written; but towards the end of the eighteenth century, when the novel had begun to succeed the drama as the dominant literary form, critics began to discuss the character of the hero, and to disagree about it. Since then there have been hundreds of different interpretations, and for many of them, incompatible as they are with one another, there seems to be some slight justification in the text of the play.

The critics fall into two main groups. The smaller group asserts that Hamlet did not delay in carrying out the task imposed upon him by the Ghost; the larger group is equally confident that Hamlet did delay, and they offer many different explanations of his procrastination.

Some of the first group say that Hamlet had to get confirmation of the Ghost's story, that he obtained this by means of the performance of 'The Murder of Gonzago', that he would have killed Claudius immediately afterwards if he had not believed that to kill a praying man would send him straight to heaven, that he had no other opportunity of carrying out his task until his encounter with the pirates and his return from his sea voyage, and that he killed the King within a few hours of his return. Some critics in this group realise that such a summary of the play is a trifle disingenuous, since it omits all mention of the soliloquies in which Hamlet blames himself for his delay, and of the months that are supposed to elapse between the appearance of the Ghost and the arrival of the Players at Elsinore, and of the Ghost's complaint on his appearance in Act III: they therefore suggest that the crucial last soliloquy was added at the time when Hamlet was changed from a youth to a man of thirty[1], or else they agree with Stoll[2] that the self-reproaches

> motive the delay, not in the sense of grounding it in character, but of explaining it, and bridging it over; they motive it by reminding the audience that the main business in hand, though retarded, is not lost to view.

Lascelles Abercrombie provided a more subtle explanation when he argued that 'those moral vacillations, for which Hamlet is so notorious, exist wholly in Hamlet's own mind'.

Most critics, however, assume on the evidence of the soliloquies, and of the Ghost's reproaches in the closet scene, that Hamlet did delay,[3] but they do not agree on his reasons for so doing. Coleridge, one of the first and most influential, argued that Hamlet was prevented from acting because he thought too much, and lost 'the power of action in the energy of resolve'. According to Goethe, 'Shakespeare sought to depict a great deed laid upon a soul unequal to the performance of it'. Bradley modified Coleridge's theory by stressing the fact that Hamlet had sustained a paralysing shock from his mother's second marriage, and that he was suffering from melancholia; and later critics have shown that Shakespeare was familiar with at least one treatise on melancholy. Schopenhauer ascribed Hamlet's delay to world-weary cynicism. Bernard Shaw argued that Hamlet half consciously revolted against the morality of revenge:

> Born into the vindictive morality of Moses he has evolved into the Christian perception of the futility and wickedness of revenge and punishment.

J. Middleton Murry ascribed Hamlet's delay partly to the command of Christ, 'Resist not evil', and partly to his sudden fear of something after death. Freud and his biographer, Ernest Jones, believed that Hamlet's delay was due to his Œdipus Complex; and Adler thinks it was rather due to his realisation that killing can be justified only in

---

[1] Jack, *op. cit.*, pp. 128 ff.   [2] Stoll, *op. cit.*, p. 94.
[3] Grebanier, however, in *The Secret of Hamlet*, points out that 'almost blunted purpose' implies that Hamlet had blunted his knife by too much use, not by too little.

self-defence. Madariaga and Rebecca West believe that Hamlet delayed because he was essentially an egotist, and in the end he avenged not his father's death, but his own.

Confronted with such divergent views,[1] the reader is likely to agree with C. S. Lewis that all these critics were describing not Hamlet, but themselves or their own pet theories.[2] It was inevitable, Lewis thinks, that Coleridge should ascribe to Hamlet his own weaknesses; it was equally inevitable that the pacifists should regard Hamlet as a pacifist, and that the Freudians should diagnose their favourite complex. To Lewis the explanation is that Hamlet is not an individual at all, but Everyman, haunted by the fear of being dead, and burdened by original sin. But Lewis's theory, ingenious as it is, invites the retort that he too, the amateur theologian, has saddled Hamlet with his own prepossessions.

Are there no objective tests we can apply to *Hamlet*, and is there no way of preventing us from analysing ourselves when we think we are portraying the character of *Hamlet*? When Caroline Spurgeon demonstrated the prevalence of sickness imagery in the play, it looked at first as though she had found a method of arriving at Shakespeare's own conception, whether conscious or unconscious, of his hero. She suggested that the disease images reflect 'not only the outward condition which causes Hamlet's spiritual illness, but also his own state'. She concluded, therefore, that Shakespeare sees Hamlet not as one unfitted by weakness of will or with too philosophic a mind to act, but suffering from 'a condition for which the individual himself is apparently not responsible'.[3] The apparent objectivity of this interpretation is deceptive, for other critics, using the same imagery as a starting-point, have arrived at different interpretations of the play. Clemen, for example, has argued that the disease imagery proliferates from the Ghost's description of the effect of Claudius's poison:

---

[1] There are many others. A certain doctor wrote an article entitled 'The Impediment of Adipose: a celebrated case'; Stekel suggests that Hamlet was Claudius's son; and another critic, on the lunatic fringe, has argued that Ham-let means Francis Bacon hindered by James I's usurpation of the English throne.

[2] C. S. Lewis, *op. cit.*   [3] C. F. E. Spurgeon, *op. cit.*, pp. 316 ff.

But this now becomes the *leitmotif* of the imagery: the individual occurrence is expanded into a symbol for the central problem of the play. The corruption of land and people throughout Denmark is understood as an imperceptible and irresistible process of poisoning.

Clemen goes on to show that the poisoning appears in the action as well, both in 'The Murder of Gonzago' and in the death of four characters in the last scene of the play. It may be added that Ophelia's madness is said to be caused by the 'poison of deep grief'. There is some difficulty in accepting this theory without modification, partly because eleven of the disease images occur before the Ghost's description of poisoning—possibly suggested by Shakespeare's knowledge of what was to come—partly because the theory tends to blur the distinction between poisoning and organic disease, and partly because it is not merely in Hamlet's imagination that the disease-imagery persists—it is used by other characters as well. But Clemen, whether right or wrong, at least illustrates the fact that the imagery can be interpreted in more ways than one.

There are two further objections to Miss Spurgeon's method. First, it is surely necessary to consider the context of the individual images. It is clear that some of the disease references are designed merely to add to the general colouring of the play, as when Claudius speaks of the defeat of England by Denmark:

> Since yet thy cicatrice looks raw and red
> After the Danish sword.

A number of the images, as we have seen, are related to the poisoning of Hamlet's father, and to the corresponding incident in 'The Murder of Gonzago'. Several of the images refer to the sickness of the state, which the audience soon realises is caused by Claudius's crime. Hamlet himself uses disease imagery again and again in relation to his uncle's guilt, as when he thinks of himself as a surgeon probing a wound ('I'll tent him to the quick') or spares the praying Claudius with the remark:

> This physic but prolongs thy sickly days.

It is true that Claudius reciprocates by using disease images about

Hamlet. He compares himself to the 'owner of a foul disease', supports his stratagem of sending Hamlet to England by the proverbial maxim that desperate diseases require drastic remedies, and refers to Hamlet's return as 'the quick of th' ulcer'. But these images surely reflect, not on Hamlet's character, but rather on Claudius's guilty fear of his nephew. Some of the disease images are used either by Hamlet or by the Queen in reference to her sin:

> It will but skin and film the ulcerous place,
> Whiles rank corruption, mining all within,
> Infects unseen.

Laertes uses three disease images, two referring to Ophelia's danger from Hamlet, and one to his hatred of Hamlet. One disease image is used to describe the futile war between Norway and Poland—'the imposthume of much wealth and peace'. It has been thought by several critics that Claudius's speech designed to strengthen Laertes's resolution to avenge his father's death is an oblique comment on Hamlet's irresolution; but neither the 'goodness, growing to a plurisy' nor the sigh 'that hurts by easing' can be directly applied to Hamlet. Nor, indeed, can Hamlet's own speech, on the way some inherited defect or some bad habit ('the dram of eale') causes people to overlook a man's virtues, be applied to the speaker, unless we find there is good reason to do so on other grounds. In any case, Hamlet is speaking of reputation, not of absolute worth. But he does use two disease images in relation to himself. As part of his pretence of madness, he tells Guildenstern that he cannot make him a wholesome answer because his wit is diseased. The other is more significant. He says that

> the native hue of resolution
> Is sicklied o'er with the pale cast of thought.

We shall have occasion to discuss the meaning of these lines in their context: their significance in the present argument is that they alone of all the passages containing sickness imagery can be plausibly used to support Miss Spurgeon's interpretation, though even here Hamlet is discussing not primarily his own weakness, but a universal phenomenon.

It is possible that the sickness imagery was suggested to Shake-speare by a famous passage in Sidney's *Defence of Poesy*. Just before his account of how a tyrant, guilty of many murders, wept at the performance of a tragedy, 'so as he that was not ashamed to make matters for *Tragedies*, yet could not resist the sweete violence of a Tragedie', Sidney describes the function of

> high and excellent *Tragedie*, that openeth the greatest woundes, and sheweth forth the *Ulcers* that are covered with *Tissue*, that maketh Kings feare to be Tyrants.

The other objection to Miss Spurgeon's method is that, by isolating a single iterative image, she has done less than justice to the imagistic complexity of the play, especially if one extends the meaning of imagery to include, as most critics now do, symbolism and iteration. The atmosphere of the play is steeped, as R. D. Altick has pointed out,[1] in the odour of corruption. Hamlet is concerned, after he has heard the Ghost's story, with what happens to the soul after death; but he seems to be equally concerned with what happens to the body. In discussing the corpse of Polonius, he comes to the conclusion that 'we fat ourselves for maggots', so that a king may 'go a progress through the guts of a beggar'. We are reminded that Polonius's corpse will stink if it is not discovered within a month. The scene in the graveyard, with Hamlet's meditations on the skulls thrown up by the gravedigger, his enquiries about 'how long a man will lie in the earth ere he rot', and his epigram on the dust of Alexander, irrelevant to the plot, are very necessary (as all producers are aware) to the atmo-sphere of the play. And these visible emblems of corruption are reinforced by numerous words and images throughout the play. There are many references to foulness and to the rankness of Clau-dius's sin. Hamlet, in his first soliloquy, wishes that his solid (or soiled) flesh would melt like dirty snow; the Ghost compares Gertrude's sin to preying on garbage; Hamlet warns Polonius of the way the sun breeds maggots in a dead dog, and tells Rosencrantz that the air seems to him 'a foul and pestilent congregation of vapours'; he com-pares Gertrude's second marriage-bed to a 'nasty sty', urges her not to 'spread the compost on the weeds To make them ranker', and

[1] *S.Q.* (1954), pp. 167-76.

speaks of 'rank corruption'. The smell of sin blends with the scent of corruption; and, contrasted with the stench of death and evil, is the perfume of flowers continually associated with Ophelia—the perfume of Hamlet's love, the flowers she distributes in her madness, the flowers she was wearing at her death, the flowers the Queen drops in her grave.

Another group of images is concerned with the cheek of the harlot, 'beautied with plastering art', which is used to symbolise hypocrisy in general as well as the falsity of women; and, since Fortune is a strumpet, it is linked with the idea of Fortune's inconstancy, and the praise of those who 'are not a pipe for Fortune's finger To sound what stop she please'. In the last act the fortune references modulate to the idea of providence, the 'divinity that shapes our ends Rough-hew them how we will', the 'special providence in the fall of a sparrow'. In one striking image, Rosencrantz compares the King with the wheel of fortune.

It is sometimes argued that the references to the child-actors, the extracts from the Dido play, and Hamlet's instructions to the Players are excrescences, even though they fill in the details of Hamlet's character, provide the occasion for one of his soliloquies, and lead up to the performance of 'The Murder of Gonzago'. But the passages concerned also link up with several themes inherent in the play. The popularity of the child actors illustrates the fickleness of public taste, and is linked by Hamlet to the flattery accorded to Claudius after he became king. The passages on the art of acting, in which Hamlet deplores ranting, are linked with his praise of Horatio, the man who is not passion's slave. Hamlet similarly praises the modesty of the Dido play and those players who do not overstep the modesty of nature. The idea that acting holds a mirror up to nature links up with Ophelia's description of Hamlet as the 'glass of fashion', with the glass Hamlet proposes to set up, in which the Queen can see her sin reflected, and with the mirror wherein alone Laertes can find his equal. There are also a number of images in the play, not directly concerned with the actors, which are derived from the theatre—prologue, 'actions that a man might play', 'perform'd at height', 'the cue for passion', 'prompted', 'bad performance', 'mutes or audience to this act'. This stage imagery, although natural to a dramatist who was also an actor, brings out the difference between appearance and reality, between the 'fiction' and the 'dream of passion' and what Wordsworth called 'the essential passions of the heart'; and it comments obliquely on what many critics regard as the central problem of the play: why it is that Hamlet can act as a madman, can take part as dramatist and even as actor in the play performed before the King, well enough to earn him 'a fellowship in a cry of players', and yet is apparently unable to perform the one action which is required of him.

There are several other groups of images which would be worth analysing—e.g. those relating to blood, to eyes and ears, and to 'discourse of reason'—but the most important group relates to war. Although Miss Spurgeon's categories may sometimes overlap, and she may have classified some of the war images differently, these would appear to outnumber those derived from sickness and medicine. Some of them are suggested by the campaigns of Hamlet's father and those of Fortinbras; others underline martial qualities, sometimes not sufficiently recognised, of the hero; but their main dramatic function is to emphasise that Claudius and Hamlet are engaged in a duel to the death. This function is particularly clear when Hamlet speaks of himself and his uncle as 'mighty opposites', between whose 'pass and fell incensed points' the luckless Rosencrantz and Guildenstern had come; but all through the play the war imagery reminds us of the struggle. Bernardo, for example, proposes to 'assail' Horatio's ears which are 'fortified against' his story; Laertes urges his sister to 'keep in the rear' of her affection, 'Out of the shot and danger of desire', and Polonius in the same scene exhorts her to set her 'entreatments at a higher rate Than a command to parle'. Later he compares the temptations of the flesh with a 'general assault'. Hamlet speaks of 'The slings and arrows of outrageous Fortune', derides the King for being 'frighted with false fire', fears that Gertrude's heart is 'proof and bulwark against sense', and boasts that he will 'delve one yard below' the mines of Rosencrantz and Guildenstern. Claudius speaks of sorrows coming 'in battalions' and compares Laertes's rebellion to 'a murdering piece' which 'in many places Gives me superfluous death'. Five of the images are taken from naval warfare (I.iii.63, III.i.112, II.ii.169, III.iv.209, V.ii.6). In addition to the war images, from which the above have been selected, there are many others which suggest violence; and together they should have the effect of counteracting some interpretations of the play, in which the psychology of the hero is the centre of interest. Equally important is the struggle between Hamlet and his uncle, Hamlet trying to prove Claudius's guilt, and Claudius, for his part, trying to pierce the secret of Hamlet's madness, and using Polonius, Rosencrantz, Guildenstern, Ophelia, and finally Gertrude as his instruments. Hamlet, in the very moment of success, reveals to Claudius the secret of his 'madness', and from that moment he knows that if he does not kill the King, the King will kill him.

It will be apparent from the above discussion that to concentrate on the sickness imagery may lead to diverse interpretations of the play, and that the imagistic structure of the play is much more complex than an isolation of this one group of images would suggest.

2.   The Play's the Thing

In the present chapter, we shall attempt to follow the action of the play and the interaction of the characters; not keeping exactly to the order of Shakespeare's scenes, because it will save repetition and recapitulation if we trace in separate sections Hamlet's relations with the different characters with whom he comes in contact. In the second section, for example, we shall follow the fortunes of Ophelia from the first act to the last.

Almost every incident in the play has been interpreted in several different ways; but although reference will occasionally be made to rival interpretations, they will generally be ignored. It seemed more useful to attempt a straightforward interpretation of the play than to engage in controversy either with living critics or with the illustrious dead.

1. The Ghost from the Grave

The first act of *Hamlet*, except for the third scene, is concerned with
the revelation by the Ghost that Claudius is a murderer and Gertrude
an adultress. This revelation is carefully prepared. The Ghost appears
twice in the first scene without speaking; and before his appearance,
Shakespeare, without the aid of scenery or artificial lighting, creates
in the course of the dialogue a vivid impression of time, place, cold-
ness, and expectancy, and after the Ghost has vanished an equally
vivid impression of dawn, four or five hours having passed in ten
minutes of playing-time. We also hear in the first scene of prepara-
tions for war, and Bernardo thinks that the Ghost has come to warn
them of the threat to the state. The scholar, Horatio, at first believes
that the Ghost will not appear, and later addresses it as 'illusion'.
According to the various beliefs current in Shakespeare's day, a
ghost could be either an illusion, 'a phantom seen as a portent of
danger to the state', a spirit come from the grave because of something
left undone, a spirit come from purgatory by divine permission, or a
devil disguised as a dead person in order to lure the living into
mortal sin.[1] All these theories are tested in the course of the play.
Horatio, abandoning the idea that the Ghost is an illusion, assumes
first that it has come as a portent and then that it can be laid if they
carry out its wishes. When the Ghost appears to Hamlet himself in
the fourth scene, both Marcellus and Horatio are afraid that it is a
goblin damned rather than a spirit of health, and that it will drive
the Prince into madness and suicide; and, although Hamlet, after he
has listened to the Ghost's message, is fully convinced that it is indeed
his father's spirit, later on he has moments of doubt when he thinks it
may be the devil. He has, in any case, to obtain confirmation of the
truth of the Ghost's story.

Hamlet appears for the first time in the second scene of the play,
dressed in black, which is an implied criticism of the royal marriage
which has just been celebrated. Claudius, although Hamlet dislikes
him and regards him as a usurper, appears to be a competent and
even an amiable ruler. After referring diplomatically to his marriage,
dispatching ambassadors to Norway, and giving Laertes permission

[1] Cf. J. Dover Wilson, *What Happens in 'Hamlet'* (1935) and J. E.
Hankins, *The Character of Hamlet* (1941), pp. 131-71.

to return to France, he urges Hamlet to stop his excessive mourning, and not to return to Wittenberg. The audience, having already seen the Ghost, is aware that something is rotten in the state of Denmark, and will sympathise with Hamlet's feelings about his mother's hasty re-marriage, especially as marriage with a deceased husband's brother was not permitted without a special dispensation.

Hamlet's first soliloquy is designed to show his state of mind before his interview with the Ghost. He is profoundly shocked by Gertrude's marriage to his uncle in less than two months after her first husband's death, although he has no conscious suspicion that his father has been murdered or that his mother had committed adultery. He wishes suicide were permissible, he compares the world to Eden after the Fall (135-7), he contrasts Gertrude's two husbands, the godlike and the bestial, and, with a tendency to generalise characteristic of him, he assumes that all women are like his mother: 'Frailty, thy name is woman!' We learn later that the melancholy and disillusionment apparent in this soliloquy are not part of his normal state of mind. It is necessary to emphasise this, because those critics who form a low opinion of his character tend to forget that his behaviour in the play is partly explicable by the successive shocks he receives.

His depression and his tears are underlined by his initial failure to recognise Horatio; but he rouses himself sufficiently to make the bitter witticism about the funeral baked meats, and his cross-examination of the three men who have seen the Ghost reveals that his intelligence has not been blunted by his grief. It is apparent from the four-line soliloquy at the end of the scene, in which he speaks of 'foul play' and 'foul deeds', that he now suspects that his father has been murdered.

In the fourth scene, before the appearance of the Ghost, Hamlet is given a speech on the drunkenness of the court, which leads him to generalise on the way 'some vicious mole of nature' or some bad habit outweighs a man's good qualities and destroys his reputation in the eyes of the world. Hamlet had already referred in the second scene to the drinking habits of the new court, and one function of this speech is to show the deterioration of Elsinore in the reign of Claudius. Another function, equally important from the theatrical point of view, is to distract the attention of the audience so that they are surprised by the reappearance of the Ghost, and this function is aided by the extreme complexity of the syntax, which would require the undivided attention of the audience.[1]

Bernard Shaw spoke of the Ghost's part as

> one of the wonders of the play. . . . The weird music of that long speech . . . should be the spectral wail of a soul's bitter wrong crying from one world to another in the extremity of its torment.

He is, apparently, released from purgatory, although Shakespeare makes use of some of the characteristics of the classical Hades. He speaks of his 'foul crimes', which suggests that Hamlet has idealised his character; and it is stressed that he has been sent to his account 'Unhous'led, disappointed, unanel'd'—without having taken the sacrament, unprepared, and without having received extreme unction. Hamlet promises to sweep to his revenge, and the Ghost leaves him with two cautions:

> Taint not thy mind, nor let thy soul contrive
> Against thy mother aught.

Gertrude is to be left to the prickings of conscience; but the meaning of the first four words of this sentence is ambiguous. They could refer to Hamlet's attitude to his mother, or they may have a more general application: he is to execute justice on Claudius, without allowing his own mind to become tainted with evil. It is important to realise that Hamlet's task is almost impossible. How can he kill Claudius in such a way that justice appears to be done, without at the same time exposing the guilt of his mother? It is apparent from the speech Hamlet utters immediately after the Ghost's disappearance that he is more concerned with his mother's guilt than with his uncle's blacker crime: he speaks first of her. It is also clear from this soliloquy and from the scene which follows that Hamlet's mind is reeling in the distracted globe of his skull. Knowing that he will be unable to behave normally till his vengeance is accomplished, he decides to 'put an antic disposition on', as Hieronimo (in *The Spanish Tragedy*) had done, or—to use a comparison made in *The Historie*

---

[1] The speech was omitted in the Folio text, and probably omitted in performance. As we have seen, it would be dangerous to follow the Olivier film in applying the words to Hamlet himself.

of Hamlet—as the Brutus who had driven out the Tarquins had done. How near to breaking-point Hamlet is after the revelation by the Ghost is made apparent by his inability to stand, by his 'wild and whirling words' to his friends, and by the hysterical remarks about the 'fellow in the cellarage', which are not a sign of his egotism and callousness as Rebecca West assumes, but which may well make his friends suspect that the Ghost is the devil in disguise. The antic disposition is not merely a defence mechanism. It also enables Hamlet to play the rôle of Fool and so make remarks which will appear mad to everyone except the guilty King, and which are a means of under-mining his self-control, so that his conscience will be caught by the performance of 'The Murder of Gonzago'.

Hamlet nearly reveals the Ghost's secret twice: first, when he breaks off to inform Horatio and Marcellus that

> There's never a villain dwelling in all Denmark
> But he's an arrant knave;

and, secondly, when he begins:

> It is an honest ghost, that let me tell you . . .

and then finishes:

> For your desire to know what is between us,
> O'ermaster it as you may.

Later on, off-stage, he makes Horatio his confidant; but he keeps the secret from Marcellus because he realises that his own safety depends on secrecy. The scene ends with a significant couplet:

> The time is out of joint. O cursed spite,
> That ever I was born to set it right!

These lines, in which Hamlet both accepts and revolts against his mission, contrast with his earlier promise to 'sweep to his revenge', and with his determination to confront the Ghost, when his fate cries out: they prepare the way for the long months of inaction.

When the Ghost appears again, in the Closet scene, it is to remind Hamlet of his unfulfilled task, and to protect Gertrude from the knowledge of Claudius's crime.

2. The Rose of May

The third scene of the play, in which Ophelia first appears, consists of three sermons. First, Laertes, who is leaving for Paris, tells Ophelia not to take Hamlet's courtship seriously, since they will not be able to marry, and above all not to let herself be seduced. Then Polonius gives some farewell advice to Laertes, mostly worldly wisdom of a not very edifying kind; and, lastly, Ophelia has to submit to a coarsely-worded sermon from her father, who assures her that the Prince's intentions are dishonourable, and that she must break off all communication with him. Ophelia is spirited enough to tell her brother to practise what he preaches, but she promises to obey her father. Some critics assume that Ophelia is not so innocent as she appears, and that she has already been seduced by Hamlet. In support of this view they point to her understanding of Hamlet's indecencies, her own song of St. Valentine's Day, and even to the possibility that she is pregnant when she is drowned. But readers of Henry James's *The Awkward Age* are aware that young girls can be acquainted with indecency without being corrupted, and Ophelia's attitude in the play-scene is perfectly compatible with innocence. She is mad when she sings of St. Valentine's Day, and it was known to Elizabethan psychologists, as well as being a stage convention, that madness frequently expressed itself in such ways. We are told by Laertes what to think of Ophelia's mad utterances:

> Thought and affliction, passion, hell itself,
> She turns to favour and to prettiness.

Nor is there any evidence that Ophelia drowned herself rather than bear an illegitimate child. 'An envious sliver broke'. But the strongest argument against such an interpretation is afforded by Hamlet's references to Ophelia. When he says that Gertrude's adultery

> takes off the rose
> From the fair forehead of an innocent love,
> And sets a blister there,

he is surely referring to Ophelia; and his curse in the nunnery scene— 'Be thou as chaste as ice, as pure as snow, thou shalt not escape calumny'—would lose its point if Ophelia were really unchaste.

Even the churlish priest allows her 'her *virgin* crants, her *maiden* strewments'.

There is some irony in the fact that although both Laertes and his father assume that the Prince cannot marry Ophelia, Gertrude (we learn later) would have welcomed the match, and there is nothing to suggest that Claudius would have disapproved.

Ophelia next appears in II.1, when she rushes in, terrified, to recount Hamlet's silent interview with her. She had repelled his letters and refused to see him, and Polonius at once assumes (as Hamlet had intended) that this has driven him mad. The scene is deliberately ambiguous. The lines used by Ophelia to describe Hamlet,

> As if he had been loosed out of hell
> To speak of horrors,

remind the audience of the Ghost's revelation, although some weeks or months have elapsed. Hamlet is putting on an antic disposition, as his state of undress makes clear, and yet his distraction may be partly real, for Ophelia's breaking with him—which he would find difficult to excuse even if he knew she did it unwillingly—seems to him to confirm his generalisation about the frailty of women. Hamlet's use of Ophelia as part of his strategy against Claudius may be explained, but not excused, by his belief that she had failed him when he most needed her; and it should weigh more heavily against him than his later indecencies and cruelties.

Ophelia's love, having been used by Hamlet, is next exploited by Claudius and her father in their attempt to find out the cause of Hamlet's 'madness'. It is not necessary to assume that Hamlet overhears Polonius's plot to 'loose' his daughter to him. Ophelia is not a good actress, and her pretence that she is reading a devotional book when she is obviously lying in wait for him, and her trite couplet—

> Take these again; for to the noble mind
> Rich gifts wax poor when givers prove unkind——

which implies that Hamlet has broken with *her*, are enough to arouse his suspicions. He suspects that Ophelia is a decoy; he tests her by asking where her father is, and, when she lies, he assumes she is on the side of the enemy, and acts the madman for the benefit of the eavesdroppers. But he lets slip a veiled threat to the listening King: 'Those that are married already, all but one, shall live.'

After Hamlet's exit, Ophelia reveals the genuineness of her love, and gives us the best picture of what Hamlet was like before the tragedy. Her former lover's pretence of madness is the first shock to her own reason, just as the appearance of Poor Tom drives Lear over the border.

Hamlet's speeches in the nunnery scene, although designed to give the impression of madness, reflect to some degree his real opinions. They express once more his disgust at the frailty of women and at their hypocrisy, symbolised by the harlot's painting, and in an obscure passage (III.i.143 ff.) he lashes their pretended innocence, which veils a secret delight in obscenity, and their use of their sex as a bait. This is one of the reasons why in the play-scene Hamlet insults Ophelia with his bawdy innuendoes. It is important to notice, however, that Hamlet does not spare himself in the nunnery-scene. He inherits corruption through his mother; and, although he may not be personally guilty of all the sins of which he accuses himself, he knows that he suffers from the taint of original sin. He is speaking for Everyman:

> Why wouldst thou be a breeder of sinners? I am myself indifferent honest, but yet I could accuse me of such things that it were better my mother had not borne me: I am very proud, revengeful, ambitious; with more offences at my beck than I have thoughts to put them in, imagination to give them shape, or time to act them in. What should such fellows as I do crawling between earth and heaven? We are arrant knaves, all; believe none of us.

His loathing of his mother's sin and of what he regards as Ophelia's betrayal leads him to self-loathing; and perhaps the cruellest thing he says to Ophelia is his denial that he had ever loved her, but only lusted after her: 'for virtue cannot so innoculate our old stock but we shall relish of it.'

Ophelia, meek and docile as she is, does not resent Hamlet's cruelty. She excuses it as a symptom of his madness, which she believes to be caused by her obedience to her father, and which she hopes her love may cure—for the Queen has hinted that she would approve of their marriage (III.i.41).

The killing of her father by the man she loves is the immediate cause of Ophelia's madness. As the King recognises, it is 'the poison of deep grief'. Laertes returns from France on hearing of Polonius's death, and Shakespeare deliberately violates probability, not letting him hear of his sister's madness until he breaks into the palace, for the sake of the dramatic poignancy of their meeting. It enables us to understand how the 'honourable' Laertes can plot to murder the man who has doubly wronged him.

The Queen's account of Ophelia's drowning (IV.vii.165 ff.) is a set piece of description, in which the favour and the prettiness are used to soften the horror. It is not particularly appropriate to the character of the Queen, and it is essentially unrealistic. She could hardly have been a spectator of the tragedy, and anyone close enough to watch the girl gradually sinking might have done something to rescue her. Nor does the account square with the gravediggers' belief that it was suicide, or with the need for a royal command to enable her to be buried in consecrated ground.

In Act V, Scene 1, the audience knows—but Hamlet and Horatio do not—that the grave is being dug for Ophelia. When Laertes leaps into the grave, Hamlet is infuriated by the ostentation, 'the bravery of his grief'. He proclaims:

> I lov'd Ophelia: forty thousand brothers
> Could not, with all their quantity of love,
> Make up my sum.

Critics disagree on the significance of this speech. Some think that Hamlet is ranting like Laertes, and that the exaggeration shows that he is being insincere. Others assume that it is a genuine expression of his former feelings for Ophelia. Both interpretations may be right; but it is significant that in his apology to Laertes just before the duel Hamlet does not mention Ophelia, and, if he accepts his responsibility for her madness and death, we are not told. He could not speak of it even to Horatio, and at this stage of the play Shakespeare could not afford a soliloquy.

The exact nature of Hamlet's feelings for Ophelia are left ambiguous. The simplest interpretation is that he loved her deeply before his mother's re-marriage, that he was compelled to give up thoughts of love when he was charged with the duty of avenging his father, and that he ceased to love her when he thought she had deserted and betrayed him. But there are things in the play which are difficult to fit in with this interpretation. The curious letter to Ophelia, which Polonius reads, is written almost in Osric's affected style. If it was written before Ophelia had refused to meet Hamlet, it is difficult to believe in the genuineness of his love. If it was written afterwards, it is strange that there is no allusion to Ophelia's apparent change of heart. If it were written after Hamlet had seen the Ghost, but before Ophelia had obeyed her father, it might be explained as part of Hamlet's strategy of madness. But it is possible that Shakespeare meant the letter to be sincere, in spite of its conceited style. Hamlet admires the old Dido play, which had to be written in an inflated style to distinguish it from the supposedly 'natural' style of *Hamlet* itself; and, in the same way, Hamlet's love-letter had to be written in a mannered style to indicate that it was a courtly composition, and different from his ordinary style of speaking.

3. The Baser Natures

Rosencrantz and Guildenstern are summoned by the King, as former schoolfellows of Hamlet, to find out the cause of his 'transformation'. They do not know that Claudius is a murderer and that Hamlet is watching for an opportunity to kill him, and they would have indignantly repudiated any idea that they were spying on a friend. Their initial motives may be perfectly respectable, even if they hope also to obtain advancement at court. But Shakespeare reveals their nullity—they are Tweedledum and Tweedledee—by the Queen's variant on the King's speech of thanks:

King. Thanks, Rosencrantz and gentle Guildenstern.
Queen. Thanks, Guildenstern and gentle Rosencrantz.

Perhaps, when Guildenstern lets slip the word 'practises', he reveals his unconscious recognition of the real nature of their task.

At first Hamlet seems genuinely glad to see them, and he cheerfully exchanges bawdy witticisms with them. But when they prick up their ears at the reference to Denmark as a prison, and try to discover whether Hamlet has been disappointed in his hopes of the crown, he suspects that they have been sent to discover the reasons for his antic disposition. His suspicion is changed to certainty when they propose to wait upon him, and he makes them confess that they were sent for. He himself explains why. He suffers from melancholia, so that the air seems to be 'a foul and pestilent congregation of vapours' and man, 'the beauty of the world, the paragon of animals', appears to be a mere 'quintessence of dust'. This speech, which is one of the most eloquent glorifications of renaissance man, and to some critics a confession of the inadequacy of man without grace, has been thought to support the view that Hamlet's delay was caused by his melancholia. There are certainly a number of verbal echoes in the play from Timothy Bright's *Treatise of Melancholy*, and Shakespeare seems to have embodied in Hamlet's character some traits of the melancholy man. But it would be hazardous to suppose that this is the whole of Hamlet's secret. We must remember that in this speech he is deliberately misleading his friends. What he says is true as far as it goes; but he naturally conceals not merely that his antic disposition is feigned, but the objective causes of his melancholy—his mother's adultery, his father's murder, and his desertion by Ophelia. Before the end of the scene, by his reference to those mockers of Claudius who now pay high prices for his portrait in miniature, Hamlet lets Rosencrantz and Guildenstern know that he does not trust them; but he tries to make amends for this remark by a ceremonious welcome.

Hamlet's next important encounter with Rosencrantz and Guildenstern is after the interruption of the play, which they suppose to be due to the Prince's insulting behaviour. Under the cloak of his antic disposition, Hamlet is offensively rude to them; he plays on their suspicion that he has been disappointed in his hopes of the crown ('Sir, I lack advancement'); and he uses the recorder as a parable of their inability to penetrate his secret: ' 'Sblood, do you think I am easier to be play'd on than a pipe?'

The King, aware now that Hamlet has guessed his secret, decides to send him to England, not as an ambassador, as he had originally intended, but as a prisoner—not for his health, but for his death. Rosencrantz and Guildenstern are detailed to be his guards. We are not told whether they know that he is being sent to execution, but their speeches about the sacredness of the King's person suggest that they would in any case have agreed to the job. Hamlet realises that Claudius must attempt to kill him, and he tells his mother that he will trust his school-fellows 'as I will adders fang'd'.

Hamlet's increasing detestation of the two men is apparent when he asks: 'Besides to be demanded of a sponge—what replication should be made by the son of a king?' Whatever the extent of their guilt, Rosencrantz and Guildenstern are certainly time-servers; and it is this which enables Hamlet, without a qualm, to hoist them with their own petard. When Horatio says, 'So Guildenstern and Rosencrantz go to't', in a tone which is presumably somewhat critical, Hamlet replies:

> Why, man, they did make love to their employment;
> They are not near my conscience; their defeat
> Does by their own insinuation grow:
> 'Tis dangerous when the baser nature comes
> Between the pass and fell incensed points
> Of mighty opposites.

It would be wrong to minimise Hamlet's callousness at this point. He is guilty of murder, and he suffers from no remorse. In mitigation it may be said that he was engaged in a secret war against his uncle, and if Rosencrantz and Guildenstern, as he assumed, knew that they were leading him to execution, he could escape only by having them killed in his place, without giving them a chance to explain, 'Not shriving time allow'd'. His action can therefore be regarded as self-defence; but his attitude to his deed shows how far he has himself been corrupted in the course of the play, as at the end of a long war humane people approve of the slaughter of the innocent.

4. What's Hecuba to him?

The play-scene is prepared for with very great care. Although *Hamlet* is Shakespeare's longest play, he felt it was necessary, or at least desirable, to preface 'The Murder of Gonzago' with a discussion of the popularity of the child actors, a puff by Polonius of the company who were visiting Elsinore, a later reference to Polonius as an amateur actor, a long extract from the Dido play, a discussion of Hamlet's proposed insertion in 'The Murder of Gonzago', an invitation to the King and Queen to attend the performance, Hamlet's advice to the players, which goes far beyond the delivery of his own speech, and his instructions to Horatio on what he is to do during the performance. Even the play itself is prefaced by a dumb-show which some critics regard as superfluous. It is worth enquiring what were Shakespeare's motives in treating these matters with such unusual amplitude. It could be argued that some passages were an artistic indulgence, if not a blunder. To an unsympathetic critic the advice to the players might seem to have been inserted because of Shakespeare's professional interest in the matter—actors, even today, are more willing to cut Hamlet's last soliloquy—and in the passage about the child actors Shakespeare's concern with the war of the theatres over-rode dramatic relevance. But, as we have seen, the topicalities are carefully linked with the main themes of the play, and there were good dramatic reasons for the apparent digressions. Shakespeare, we may suppose, wished to make Hamlet a more rounded character than would otherwise be possible. We see him at the beginning of the play in what is for him an unusual suicidal mood, and we never have a chance, except in retrospective comments, of seeing him as he was before his mother's remarriage; and so his long-standing interest in the theatre, his courteous reception of the players, his obviously sensible views on acting, his less obviously sensible taste in drama, his ability as an amateur actor and dramatist all bear out the truth of Ophelia's tribute to his gifts—

The courtier's, soldier's, scholar's eye, tongue, sword.

There was another reason for the leisurely treatment of these scenes. The action of the first act had been rapid; but in the second act, and in part of the third, it was essential to give an effect of stagnation. By the time of the performance of 'The Murder of Gonzago' four months had elapsed since the murder of Hamlet's father; the action of the second and third acts is almost continuous,[1] so that we must suppose that more than two months have passed since Hamlet

[1] 'The Murder of Gonzago' is performed on the day after the arrival of the players.

had vowed that he would sweep to his revenge. He has done nothing, and bitterly reproaches himself for having done nothing. The stagnation of the action is a reflection of Hamlet's apparent impotence. At last, with the arrival of the players, he sees a chance of testing the truth of the Ghost's story: for by now he has either begun to doubt it, or is at least aware that he must, if he is not to seem a murderer anxious to seize the crown, obtain confirmatory evidence. We see the birth of his plot and we watch the laying of the trail and the setting light to the fuse before the great dramatic climax when Claudius calls for lights, both to interrupt the play and to lighten his darkness. The effect is carefully prepared. We see the effect of the Dido play on Hamlet himself; we are told that 'the purpose of playing is to hold, as it were, a mirror up to nature'; that

> Guilty creatures, sitting at a play,
> Have by the very cunning of the scene
> Been struck so to the soul that presently
> They have proclaim'd their malefactions;

and that Hamlet believes that Claudius's 'occulted guilt' will 'itself unkennel in one speech'. We watch Hamlet's anxiety that the crucial speech shall be delivered as naturally as possible, so that it will make its full effect; and we catch the infection of Hamlet's excitement immediately before the performance.

Hamlet's praise of the Dido play which was 'caviary to the general' and which had 'no matter in the phrase which might indict the author of affectation' has been explained in various ways. We can either assume that the Prince's taste was odd; or we can take the words as a tribute to Marlowe who wrote the Dido play which served Shakespeare as a model; or we can suppose that Shakespeare, on first looking into Chapman's Homer, had thought that the style he employed here, in parts of *Troilus and Cressida*, and in the second scene of *Macbeth*, was proper for epic narration; or, finally, he may have realised that the style of the extract had to differ from that of the rest of the play as it was further from reality. These explanations are not mutually exclusive.

Hamlet chooses this particular passage, whether consciously or unconsciously, because Pyrrhus is the ruthless king-killer Claudius

had been, the ruthless avenger he wished to be himself. The
where Pyrrhus stands with his sword suspended over the head of
Priam is echoed later in the play when Hamlet stands over the kneel-
ing Claudius. The curse on the 'strumpet Fortune' echoes what
Hamlet himself had said, in a lighter key, earlier in this scene.
Hecuba's mourning for her husband is contrasted with Gertrude's
brief mourning for hers. In the soliloquy that follows, Hamlet contrasts the actor's ability to weep tears for an imaginary sorrow with
his own inability not merely to do anything, but to say anything.
He works himself up into an hysterical passion of hatred against
Claudius, and then breaks down in an agony of self-disgust. There
follows his scheme to catch the conscience of the King:

> I'll have these players
> Play something like the murder of my father
> Before mine uncle.

As he has already asked the First Player if he will memorise a speech
to be inserted in 'The Murder of Gonzago', it is obvious that he has
not just thought of the plot. The whole soliloquy, indeed, is a 'dis-
placed aside'. It tells us what had been passing through Hamlet's
mind during the recitation of the speeches from the Dido play.

After the excitement of this soliloquy, and the mood of determination with which it ends, it is a shock to find Hamlet, on his appearance
in the very next scene, apparently toying with thoughts of suicide;
and there is a further shock when, after his hysterical outburst against
Ophelia, we find him a few minutes later quietly instructing the
professional actors on the technique of their art. This violent oscilla-
tion of mood, which is to be found in several other places in the play,
has to be reckoned with in any attempt to discuss Hamlet's character.
A modern psychologist might label him as a 'manic depressive', but
the actual phenomenon was one with which Timothy Bright was
perfectly familiar.

5. The Name of Action

It is, in fact, debatable whether Hamlet was really discussing suicide
in the 'To be or not to be' soliloquy. The speech has suffered from
being detached from its context: it is spoken, that is, between the

time when Hamlet has laid his plot and the actual performance of the play. In the opening lines, as Johnson realised, Hamlet is not discussing whether to kill himself or not, but whether to kill Claudius or not, if the play proves his guilt. This is made clear from the way in which he expands the opening words. The alternatives are not endurance of life or suicide, but

> Whether 'tis nobler in the mind to suffer
> The slings and arrows of outrageous fortune,
> Or to take arms against a sea of troubles,
> And by opposing end them——

whether to endure the reign of the usurping murderer and the whoring of his mother, or to attempt to kill Claudius. The attempt may, probably will, cost him his own life; so, without a break—in the Quarto there is only a comma after *them*—he goes on to think of the felicity of escaping from

> the thousand natural shocks
> That flesh is heir to. 'Tis a consummation
> Devoutly to be wish'd.

But if death is a sleep, sleep may be accompanied by nightmares. Even his father, as he has cause to remember, although a good man and a good king, was being tortured in purgatory for his 'foul crimes'; and the secrets of his prison-house were too horrible to be revealed to ears of flesh and blood. No wonder, then, that Everyman chooses to endure the miseries of a long life rather than invite by the sin of suicide worse miseries in

> The undiscover'd country, from whose bourn
> No traveller returns.

It has been suggested that these words show that Hamlet no longer believes that his father had come from the grave; but he might well distinguish between the return of a spirit and the return of a Lazarus in flesh and blood. At this point he is speaking not primarily of himself, but of every man, as the generalised list of human miseries indicates:[1]

---

[1] Shakespeare himself gives a similar list in Sonnet 66.

Th' oppressor's wrong, the proud man's contumely,
The pangs of dispriz'd love, the law's delay,
The insolence of office, and the spurns
That patient merit of th' unworthy takes.

Thus, Hamlet continues to generalise, 'conscience does make cowards of us all'. Some critics assume that by *conscience* Hamlet means 'thinking too precisely on th' event' or else the 'craven scruple' of which he speaks in his last soliloquy. But it seems more likely that Hamlet is using the word as he does elsewhere in the play ('the conscience of the King', 'perfect conscience') in the ordinary modern sense. Man's 'dread of something after death', the pains of hell or purgatory, prevent him from committing suicide. Hamlet had earlier declared that 'to be honest as this world goes is to be one man picked out of ten thousand', and he tells Ophelia later in this scene:

I am myself indifferent honest, but yet I could accuse me of such things that it were better my mother had not borne me. . . . What should such fellows as I do crawling between earth and heaven?

Even if we assume that he is exaggerating, there is enough truth here to make him afraid of death and judgment after death; and we may remember that in *Measure for Measure* another young man decided that

The weariest and most loathed worldly life
That age, ache, penury, and imprisonment
Can lay on nature is a paradise
To what we fear of death.

Hamlet, therefore, since his enterprise of 'great pitch and moment' against the King may well involve his own death, naturally hesitates:

And thus the native hue of resolution
Is sicklied o'er with the pale cast of thought.

The implication is that although it is nobler to kill the King than to refrain from vengeance, Hamlet is answering the question in his previous soliloquy, 'Am I a coward', in the affirmative. He is not afraid of dying, but of what may happen after death. Yet, such is the ambiguity with which Shakespeare presents the character, we do not know whether Hamlet is right about himself, or whether it is but

another example of the self-laceration in which he indulges because
of his delay in carrying out his task.

In the dialogue with Horatio, Hamlet disinterestedly praises the
man who, unlike the Everyman of the soliloquy, has been

> As one, in suff'ring all, that suffers nothing;
> A man that Fortune's buffets and rewards
> Hast ta'en with equal thanks; and blest are those
> Whose blood and judgment are so well comeddled
> That they are not a pipe for Fortune's finger
> To sound what stop she please. Give me that man
> That is not passion's slave, and I will wear him
> In my heart's core, ay, in my heart of heart,
> As I do thee.

Those critics who over-stress Hamlet's pride and egotism overlook
the significance of these lines. Hamlet's admiration for Horatio is
whole-hearted and generous. He admires him for the qualities he
feels to be lacking in himself; and the speech should be read in conjunction with Hamlet's self-condemnation at the end of the second
act:

> Why, what an ass am I! This is most brave,
> That I, the son of a dear father murder'd,
> Prompted to my revenge by heaven and hell,
> Must, like a whore, unpack my heart with words,
> And fall a-cursing like a very drab.

It should be read, too, in conjunction with the scene immediately
before the one with Horatio, when Hamlet's wholesale attack on
women reveals him once again as passion's slave. But we should
remember also Hamlet's question to Guildenstern after the play:
' 'Sblood, do you think I am easier to be play'd on than a pipe?'

Horatio is very like the Senecal man described by Chapman in a
play that might almost have been written as an answer to *Hamlet*:
The Revenge of Bussy D'Ambois. Clermont is called upon to avenge
his brother's death, and he accepts the duty unflinchingly. He indulges
in no self-accusations; he does not feign madness; and he is scrupulous about the means he employs. He sends a challenge to his enemy,
which is declined. Later on, he has doubts about the Ghost, and he
regrets that he has agreed to avenge his brother's death since 'private

cause' should not assume the function of 'public laws'. But the Ghost reappears and reminds him that he must supply 'What corrupted law Leaves unperform'd.' Clermont, therefore, slays his enemy in fair fight, without anger or hatred, and speaks of him as 'worthy soul'. At one point of the play Clermont is criticised for not murdering his enemy as he deserves; but he refuses to 'revenge a villany with villany'. 'We must wreak our wrongs', he declares, 'So we take not more'. When he hears that his friend, Guise, has been murdered by the King, he at once distinguishes between legitimate revenge and the impious revenge on the sacred person of a king. He therefore commits suicide, so as to escape 'all the horrors of the vicious time'. Clermont is an ideal and idealised hero. He behaves as Seneca in his essays exhorted men to behave, and as we may suppose Horatio would behave in a similar situation. He bears good and evil fortune with equal calm:

> In short, this Senecal man is found in him,
> He may with heaven's immortal powers compare,
> To whom the day and fortune equal are;
> Come fair or foul, whatever chance can fall,
> Fixed in himself, he still is one to all.

Chapman, as several critics have pointed out, would have despised the character of Hamlet. He would have thought that the intermingling of great qualities with obvious defects could not provide that 'material instruction, elegant and sententious excitation to virtue, and deflection from her contrary' which was the purpose of tragedy. He would not have approved of the way Hamlet becomes partially corrupted by the deed he has to do, or of the way his very reluctance involves him more deeply in the mire. But whereas Chapman's play presents an ideal, Shakespeare's gives us an image of reality. Hamlet was in a situation where the use of scrupulous means was literally impossible; and, although Horatio's virtues show up Hamlet's weaknesses, he would not make a satisfactory hero of a tragedy.

6. The Conscience of the King

Hamlet, in the play-scene, chooses to sit at Ophelia's feet rather than next to the Queen, partly to encourage the idea that his madness is caused by disappointed love, but mainly because he could not watch the King's face if he sat next to the royal pair. The dumb-show is the first part of the King's ordeal. He can hardly stop the play before it has properly begun; he hopes that it is an unlucky coincidence that 'The Murder of Gonzago' resembles his own crime, but he naturally suspects that the choice of play is deliberate, and he knows that Hamlet is watching his reactions. He asks later, 'Have you heard the argument? Is there no offence in 't?' As the remarks about second marriages, which he has heard, are grossly offensive, he pretends not to have noticed them. There is a purely practical reason for the dumb-show.[1] As the play is stopped before the end, Shakespeare has to inform the audience of the plot.

'The Murder of Gonzago', with its deliberately artificial style, full of repetitions and circumlocutions, enables us to concentrate on the real drama which is being enacted, with Hamlet's eyes riveted on his uncle's face, with the Queen painfully embarrassed, with the courtiers scandalised, and with the King trying hard not to show by his face what he is feeling. The words of the Player Queen emerge with dreadful clarity from the surrounding verbiage:

> In second husband let me be accurst!
> None wed the second but who kill'd the first . . .
> A second time I kill my husband dead,
> When second husband kisses me in bed . . .
> Both here and hence pursue me lasting strife,
> If, once a widow, ever I be wife.

Hamlet by his interjections makes it certain that the point shall be understood: 'That's wormwood, wormwood' . . . 'If she should break it now!' . . . 'O, but *she*'ll keep her word'.

There are other passages in the play which link up with the main themes of *Hamlet*. The Player King reminds his Queen, and may remind Hamlet too, that

[1] J. D. Wilson thinks that Hamlet is annoyed by the dumb-show, which he had not expected, because he is afraid it will put the King on his guard ('The players cannot keep counsel; they'll tell all'). Others have suggested that the dumb-show was intended as an alternative to the play; but we know from Q1 that both were given on Shakespeare's stage.

> Purpose is but the slave to memory,
> Of violent birth, but poor validity . . .
> The violence of either grief or joy
> Their own enactures with themselves destroy.

In the same speech he has a passage on Fortune, and another on the way fate intervenes in human affairs:

> Our wills and fates do so contrary run
> That our devices still are overthrown;
> Our thoughts are ours, their ends none of our own.

One line, which has been thought to refer to the fall of Essex, is more likely to have a general application:

> The great man down, you mark his favourite flies.

After the exit of the Player Queen, Claudius appears to be cowed. Hamlet's assertion that the play is entitled 'The Mouse-trap' is a veiled threat of which the King is perfectly aware, especially as 'mouse' is his term of endearment for Gertrude. When Lucianus enters, Hamlet's comment that he is 'nephew to the King' could be taken as another threat, and his anxiety about the melodramatic acting of the player with his 'damnable faces' may indicate that Lucianus's lines are the ones he himself has written; but they seem to be less effective for the purpose than the lines quoted above from the part of the Player Queen. Claudius, watching for a second time the re-enactment of his crime, is at breaking-point; and when Hamlet gives a last twist to the knife by explaining, 'You shall see anon how the murderer gets the love of Gonzago's wife', the King rises, 'frighted with false fire'. Hamlet has confirmed the Ghost's story, but at the expense of revealing his knowledge to the King. His own fate is sealed unless he follows up his victory. This victory is imperfect, in any case, because Hamlet's behaviour during the performance, as well as the apparent gross lack of taste in his choosing a play with such a theme, can allow the King to cover up his guilt with a show of anger.

At the end of the scene Hamlet is left to soliloquise on his readiness to do the 'bitter business' required of him. But he has first to see his mother, and he cautions himself against matricide—Nero killed his mother—not, presumably, because he was ever so tempted, but as a hint to the audience that he 'will speak daggers to her, but use none', On the way to his mother's closet—which modern producers often transform into a bedroom so as to underline a Freudian interpretation —Hamlet discovers that he has indeed caught the conscience of the King: Claudius is on his knees. He has spoken before of the heavy burden of his sin, so that the spectacle is not altogether unexpected. But although he knows that he cannot be pardoned and retain the offence, he is not prepared to give up the fruits of his crime: his words fly up, his thoughts remain below.

This is Hamlet's first opportunity of killing his uncle: but his opening words are in the subjunctive mood: 'Now *might* I do it pat'. He finally decides to spare Claudius because he remembers that his father's 'foul crimes' are being expiated in purgatory, and it would be an inadequate revenge to send his murderer to heaven. He wishes to damn his uncle's soul, not merely to slay his body. Shakespeare underlines the irony by showing immediately after Hamlet's speech that Claudius was unable to pray.

This episode will be interpreted according to our general view of Hamlet's character; or, to put it the other way round, our interpretation of Hamlet will very largely depend on our interpretation of this episode. Do we take Hamlet's reasons for not killing the King at their face value, and shall we be as much revolted by them as Johnson was? Or, shall we assume, with Coleridge and Bradley, that the wish to send Claudius to hell was an afterthought, offered by Hamlet to excuse his own failure to act? (such critics can point to the tell-tale *might* in the first line of the speech). Or, shall we suppose that Hamlet has an instinctive revulsion from killing a defenceless man at the foot of an altar, and then, revolting against his own revulsion, works himself up into a passion of hatred which provides him with a substitute for action, as in the soliloquy at the end of the second act? The desire to damn one's enemy, body and soul, is characteristic of the revenge play; but Shakespeare may be using a commonplace for more sophisticated purposes.

7. Scourge and Minister

Polonius meets his death while hiding behind the arras to spy on the interview between Hamlet and Gertrude. The fate is not inappropriate for one who had sent Reynaldo to spy on Laertes in Paris, and virtually to act as *agent provocateur*, especially if, as several passages suggest, he had helped Claudius to get the crown. The fact that Polonius is Hamlet's butt throughout the play, his own long-winded speeches, his tedious moralising which screens his unscrupulous behaviour, and his gross errors of judgment with regard to Hamlet and Ophelia, may persuade us to write him off as a tedious old fool, 'declining into dotage', as Johnson observed. But he is a pillar of Elsinore society, respected both by Claudius and Gertrude; and if he is not so clever as he thinks, he is cleverer than he seems.

Hamlet's prompt killing of Polonius contrasts with his refusal to kill Claudius a few minutes before. He thinks, of course, that it is Claudius behind the arras, a Claudius no longer in sanctuary but engaged in an act that 'has no relish of salvation in't'. Claudius is bound to seek Hamlet's life, even though he is 'loved of the distracted multitude'; and Hamlet, apart from his duty of revenge, must kill Claudius now in self-defence. He is able to do the deed because he does not have time to think about it. His cry of 'A rat?' recalls 'The Mousetrap'.

Rebecca West and others call the killing of Polonius 'murder'; but, as Hamlet thought he was killing Claudius, the verdict is harsh. It is true that his epitaph on his victim is perfunctory and callous:

> Thou wretched, rash, intruding fool, farewell!
> I took thee for thy better. Take thy fortune:
> Thou find'st to be too busy is some danger.

Later on, he says, 'For this same lord, I do repent'; but his last reference to the matter is: 'I'll lug the guts into the neighbour room.' Yet the Queen tells Claudius that Hamlet weeps for his deed, and this is more likely to be the truth than an invention to shield her son. It seems probable that Shakespeare intended the callousness of Hamlet's remarks to be a cover to his real feelings, or at least that they represent a temporary mood which alternates with one of repentance.

The speeches in which Hamlet tries to bring his mother to repentance have likewise been interpreted in different ways. On the one hand, critics have regarded them as intolerably self-righteous, exaggerating Gertrude's guilt, and taking an obscene pleasure in depicting her lust in action, almost as though Hamlet were jealous. On the other hand, it is pointed out that it is Hamlet's duty to bring his mother to repentance, that he determines beforehand to 'speak daggers to her', that he apologises later that he has had to 'be cruel only to be kind', and that he does in fact succeed in making his mother repent and in winning her to his side. The means he uses are harsh, but they are justified by his success. When he apologises ironically for his virtue——

> Forgive me this my virtue;
> For in the fatness of these pursy times
> Virtue itself of vice must pardon beg,
> Yea, curb and woo for leave to do him good——

the Elizabethans would not have thought that Hamlet was being self-righteous, any more than they would have thought Othello boastful when he declares that he has 'done the state some service'.

The truth lies, perhaps, somewhere between these two interpretations. There is no reason to think that in his savage attack on his mother's sin Hamlet was disobeying the Ghost's injunction not to contrive anything against his mother. Even if he was not literally leaving her to heaven and the stings of conscience, it was certainly not violating the spirit of the Ghost's instructions to stimulate the workings of conscience. Until this scene Gertrude seems to be unaware that she has done anything wrong. But the Ghost's other injunction, that Hamlet should not taint his mind, he has not been able to obey; for Gertrude's adultery

> blurs the grace and blush of modesty;
> Calls virtue hypocrite; takes off the rose
> From the fair forehead of an innocent love,
> And sets a blister there; makes marriage-vows
> As false as dicers' oaths. O, such a deed
> As from the body of contraction plucks
> The very soul, and sweet religion makes
> A rhapsody of words.

Because of this, Hamlet's attitude to sex, and to life as a whole, been tainted. If Bradley is right in describing *Hamlet* as a 'tragedy of moral idealism', it should be added that a disillusioned idealism often ends in cynicism and morbidity. There is, indeed, something morbid about the way Hamlet wallows in the picture of his mother

> In the rank sweat of an enseamed bed,
> Stew'd in corruption, honeying and making love
> Over the nasty sty!

or in his fear that the 'bloat king' will tempt her again to bed, and for 'a pair of reechy kisses' give away the secret of Hamlet's madness. There is one slight indication (IV.vii.111 ff.) that Gertrude does withdraw herself from her husband, although she tries to protect him from Laertes's attack. But for Hamlet to succeed in awakening some sense of sin in the moral defective, Gertrude, was a triumph. He does it by a verbal portrait of her two husbands, and by a vivid and repulsive series of pictures of the realities of middle-aged sexual appetite, the rebellious hell that mutinies in a matron's bones. He seems about to reveal that Claudius had murdered his brother when the Ghost appears, not in armour, but in his habit as he lived, presumably to prevent this revelation. Hamlet alone sees the Ghost, and the meaning of this is disputed. Some have argued that the Ghost in this scene is an hallucination, since he is not visible to the Queen, and since his message—not to forget the duty of revenge and to comfort Gertrude—reflects only Hamlet's thoughts. But others have rightly argued that Gertrude cannot see her former husband because she has betrayed him.

In speaking of the death of Polonius, Hamlet declares:

> Heaven hath pleas'd it so,
> To punish me with this, and this with me,
> That I must be their scourge and minister.

Fredson Bowers[1] has shown that 'scourge' and 'minister' were not synonymous terms. A scourge, such as Tamburlaine, 'the scourge of God', was a wicked man who heaped further damnation on himself by his career of crime, even though he was used by Providence to

---

[1] F. Bowers, *P.M.L.A.*, lxx (1950), pp.740-7.

punish the sins of others. This was why King James could argue that it was never right to rebel even against a wicked king. A minister, on the other hand, was chosen by God as His instrument to execute a particular justice; and God, in His own good time, would provide a suitable opportunity. Hamlet had not yet been given an opportunity —for murdering a praying man could hardly be regarded as that— and he had already been the cause of the death of one innocent person. Before the end of the play five more people were to die, apart from Claudius. At this point in the play, with Claudius alive and Polonius slain, Hamlet was bound to wonder whether 'scourge' or 'minister' were his rôle.

8. Hamlet's Heir

When the play opens, the state of Denmark is threatened, not merely by the hidden rottenness of an unpunished murder, but also by war. The elder Fortinbras had been killed in single combat by the elder Hamlet, and young Fortinbras is determined to avenge his father's death by recovering the lands that his death had forfeited. He is acting without the knowledge of his uncle, the King of Norway; and his army is a gang of adventurers, 'a list of lawless resolutes' which he has 'shark'd up'. Denmark is therefore preparing for war, as we hear in the first scene of the play, but Claudius sends ambassadors to Norway to demand that Fortinbras should be stopped (I.ii). The ambassadors are successful in their mission, and Claudius in return gives permission for Fortinbras's troops to pass through Denmark on their way to attack Poland (II.ii.). These troops duly appear (IV.iv.) and we learn that they

> go to gain a little patch of ground
> That hath in it no profit but the name.

In the last scene of the play, Fortinbras returns in triumph from Poland, in time to claim the Danish throne, now vacant through the deaths of Claudius and Hamlet.

Fortinbras, in some sense, is a foil to Hamlet. He sets out to avenge his father's death, and he succeeds, not merely in recovering the lost lands, but in annexing a part of Poland for which he has no legitimate

claim, and in obtaining the throne of his father's old enemy. Hamlet
moreover, believing that he will make a successful king, gives him
his dying voice.

The two princes do not actually meet—Fortinbras leaves the stage
as Hamlet enters with Rosencrantz and Guildenstern—but Hamlet
discusses with the realistic Captain the futile war on which Fortinbras
is engaged. He describes it as

> th' imposthume of much wealth and peace,
> That inward breaks, and shows no cause without
> Why the man dies.

In spite of this bitter comment, Hamlet in the last of his soliloquies
uses Fortinbras's behaviour as a criticism of his own. He is on his way
to England, from which he may never return; he has exposed the
guilt of the King, but spared his life; by killing Polonius he has put
himself in the power of his enemy and turned Laertes into a ruthless
avenger; and, if he ever returns to Denmark, his chances of catching
the King off his guard are small indeed. Hamlet blames himself, not
as Coleridge did, for thinking too much, but for allowing 'capability
and god-like reason' to fust in him unused. He professes not to know
why he has not carried out his task:

> Now, whether it be
> Bestial oblivion, or some craven scruple
> Of thinking too precisely on th' event—
> A thought which, quarter'd, hath but one part wisdom
> And ever three parts coward—I do not know
> Why yet I live to say 'This thing's to do',
> Sith I have cause, and will, and strength, and means
> To do't.

He is, of course, deceiving himself. At this stage of the play he has
neither the strength nor the means to avenge his father, and the cause
and the will are useless without the rest. He is really thinking of the
months that have elapsed since he was charged with the killing of
the King, and of the way his revenge has slipped through his fingers.
In future he intends to brush aside craven scruples, and to abandon
'thinking too precisely on th' event', which means in effect to jettison
the reason which alone distinguishes man from the beasts. Fortinbras

and his troops risk their lives for 'an egg-shell' and 'find quarrel in a straw', ostensibly when honour is at stake, but in reality for 'a fantasy and trick of fame'. Hamlet proposes to follow the barbarous example of the 'delicate and tender prince', and so be able to carry out his task:

> O, from this time forth,
> My thoughts be bloody, or be nothing worth!

Fortinbras is a foil, and Hamlet uses him as a spur. It is natural that at the nadir of his fortunes, Hamlet should contrast Fortinbras's single-minded pursuit of his ambition with his own failure to carry out a task which he regarded as a cursed spite. It was natural, too, that he should feel that his honour was besmirched by his failure to kill Claudius, even though honour and justice were at odds. All through the play, Hamlet, like his creator, is

> Desiring this man's art, and that man's scope.

He would like to exchange the qualities he has for the coarser qualities which would have brought him success.

9. Hamlet's Foil

Laertes, like Fortinbras and Horatio, is Hamlet's foil; and his situation in the second half of the play is very like Hamlet's own. Hamlet has a father killed and a mother stained, and he has the task of vengeance imposed upon him by the ghost of his father; Laertes has a father killed, he is afraid that his sister will be stained, and she is driven mad—and the culprit in both cases is the avenger of the main plot.

Laertes, like Hamlet, has come to Elsinore for Claudius's coronation; he wishes to return to France, as Hamlet wishes to return to Wittenberg. The two men are on the stage at the same time, but they do not speak to each other. In the next scene Laertes warns Ophelia against Hamlet, apparently believing that he will try to seduce her. Ophelia, aware of the double standard for men and women, mildly retorts that she hopes he will practise what he preaches. Laertes, in his turn, has to listen to a sermon from his father. In the very revealing scene between Polonius and Reynaldo, it is clear that they both expect Laertes to be a bit of a rake. Polonius's method of extracting information about his son reveals a lack of trust and a coarseness of fibre in the father, and it suggests that, compared with Hamlet, Laertes is less idealistic and more easy-going in his morals.

Laertes returns from Paris on receiving the news of his father's death. Although it is obvious that he is not so devoted to his father as Hamlet was to his, he immediately takes steps to avenge Polonius's death, raises a rebellion, storms the palace, and has Claudius at his mercy. We are meant to understand that the more popular Prince could have done the same.

One has the feeling that Laertes knows exactly how he should react to every situation, according to the conventional views of the time, and that he behaves accordingly. It was the natural result of being brought up in a house where 'what is done' was always more important than what ought to be done. When, for example, the Queen urges him to be calm, he bursts out:

> That drop of blood that's calm proclaims me bastard;
> Cries cuckold to my father. . . .

The rhetorical over-emphasis, apparent also in the graveyard scene, shows how even his initial sincerity becomes vulgarised.

The King has no difficulty in persuading Laertes that he is not to blame for Polonius's death, and he is about to tell him of the news he is expecting from England, when letters arrive from Hamlet himself, and he knows that his plot has failed. Immediately, he begins another plot, casting Laertes as the chief actor. He approaches the subject very gingerly, but when Laertes declares that he would cut Hamlet's throat in the church, the King realises that he need not have been so careful; and we are reminded of the way Hamlet would not kill the King while he was praying. The plot requires that Hamlet shall not peruse the foils, and Claudius admits that his intended victim is 'Most generous, and free from all contriving'. This plot has the advantage that the Queen might suppose that the unbated foil was an accident; but Laertes nullifies this advantage, even though it makes Hamlet's death more certain, by proposing to anoint his sword with poison. To buy poison in case of need exhibits a deeper depravity in

Laertes than he has yet revealed; and it is this refinement which is the cause of his own death. The King, who has used poison before, decides to provide a poisoned chalice in case Hamlet escapes the 'venom'd stuck'; but, as Macbeth reminds us, 'even-handed justice Commends the ingredience of our poison'd chalice To our own lips'. The murderous pact is sealed by the news of Ophelia's death.

The next time we see Laertes, at the grave of his sister, Hamlet calls him with unconscious irony 'a very noble youth'. But he regains some sympathy by his exchange with the churlish priest, and does not entirely lose it when he leaps into the grave and asks to be buried alive. But, here again, Laertes is going beyond what he really feels, as Hamlet is quick to recognise. This is the first time that Shakespeare brings the two men face to face. Hamlet has only just learnt that Ophelia is dead, that the Queen hoped they would marry, that his killing of her father had led to her madness, and to her death; and, though he rants to outface Laertes, he convinces us that he loved her more than one brother, if not more than forty thousand. The encounter by the grave of the woman they both loved confirms Laertes in his resolution to murder Hamlet. Yet, when it comes to the point, he is ashamed of what he is doing. In answer to Hamlet's apology that he had 'shot his arrow o'er the house' and hurt his brother (as Laertes would have been if Hamlet had married Ophelia), Laertes says that although he will not be officially reconciled until his case has been considered by a tribunal, he will nevertheless receive Hamlet's 'offer'd love like love, And will not wrong it'.

When Laertes asks for a foil, Hamlet quibbles on the word:

> I'll be your foil, Laertes; in mine ignorance
> Your skill shall, like a star i' th' darkest night,
> Stick fiery off indeed.

But Laertes, as we have seen, is a foil to Hamlet in another sense.

We may suppose that Laertes's guilty conscience prevents him from displaying the skill of which Lamord had spoken, for Hamlet scores the first two hits. At last, almost against his conscience, Laertes attacks Hamlet before he is ready and scores the necessary hit. Hamlet, although not realising the full extent of the treachery, disarms Laertes and secures the unbated rapier. Laertes is wounded before the

King can intervene, and admits that he has met his deserts. In his dying moments he reveals the King's villainy and exchanges forgiveness with Hamlet.

Laertes is the ruthless avenger that Hamlet, with half his mind, wishes to be; and he throws into relief the hesitations and craven scruples of the hero. He is almost what some of Hamlet's critics blame him for not being, and he might almost have been put into the play to show them how wrong they were. 'By the image of my cause', Hamlet told Horatio earlier, 'I see the portraiture of his'. It is one measure of the gulf between the two avengers that Laertes could never have used these words about Hamlet.

10. Special Providence

The hero of *Fratricide Punished* escapes the plot to murder him in England by tricking his attendants into shooting each other. Hamlet is saved (as he believes) by

> a divinity that shapes our ends
> Rough-hew them how we will,

which enables him to find the King's commission in the dark. Heaven was ordinant, too, in providing him with his father's signet, with which to seal the forged commission, and with a pirate-ship to take him back to Denmark. Although on his return to Elsinore Hamlet seems further away than ever from the fulfilment of his task, since Claudius has tried to kill him once and will again, he has now ceased to indulge in self-reproaches, presumably because he is confident that the providence which has preserved him will provide him with his opportunity. He knows now he is a minister and not a scourge.

The interest he displays in the mysteries of grave-making, the elegiac speech on Yorick, and even the injunction to the skull to tell my lady 'let her paint an inch thick, to this favour she must come', are without bitterness; and just as the reference to cosmetics may be contrasted with his earlier words to Ophelia, so the meditation on the dust of Alexander may be contrasted with the bitterer demonstration of the way a king may go a progress through the guts of a beggar. He broods on death because he has a premonition of his own.

He is shocked out of his calm by the revelation that the new grave is for Ophelia, and that he himself is ultimately responsible for her death; but, when he comes forward, his announcement of himself has a new authority: 'This is I, Hamlet the Dane.' When Laertes attacks him, his parody of his enemy's rhetorical grief can be interpreted by the Queen as madness, and Hamlet remembers on his exit to put on his antic disposition for the last time:

> Let Hercules himself do what he may,
> The cat will mew, and dog will have his day.

In the next scene, Hamlet describes to Horatio how he forged the commission and sent Rosencrantz and Guildenstern to their deaths, and he makes a final statement of Claudius's crimes—the killing of his father, the whoring of his mother, the seizure of the throne, and the attempt on his own life—and he asks Horatio:

> Is't not perfect conscience
> To quit him with this arm? And is't not to be damn'd
> To let this canker of our nature come
> In further evil?

Horatio reminds Hamlet that he must act before news arrives from England 'What is the issue of the business there'. Hamlet replies confidently: 'The interim is mine'.

The satirical scene with Osric which follows—necessary, perhaps, on Shakespeare's stage to enable the trap for Ophelia's grave to be closed—provides a last picture of the decadence of the Danish court (with its decadent style) and the details of the wager. Hamlet is confident of winning at the odds. His statement that he has been in continual practice since Laertes went into France conflicts with his earlier remark (II.ii.296) that he had 'forgone all custom of exercises'; but this passes unnoticed in the theatre. Once again he has a premonition of his own death, but he refuses to postpone the duel:

> Not a whit, we defy augury: there is a special providence in the fall
> of a sparrow. If it be now, 'tis not to come; if it be not to come, it
> will be now; if it be not now, yet it will come—the readiness is all.

This is not the stoical fatalism, which it has seemed to be to some critics, but, as the Biblical reference to the fall of a sparrow makes clear, a trust in providence. It contrasts, in this respect, with Edgar's words in *King Lear*, where the Christian reference would be anachronistic:

> Men must endure
> Their going hence, even as their coming hither:
> Ripeness is all.

Hamlet's apology to Laertes has been condemned by critics who think it is disingenuous of him to pretend that he killed Polonius in a fit of madness; but he can hardly tell Laertes that he intended to kill the King. In a few minutes the four chief characters in the play are dead: Laertes is caught as a woodcock in his own springe—his father had described Hamlet's vows to Ophelia as 'springes to catch woodcocks'; Gertrude dies, knowing that the poisoned cup was intended for her son and realising that Claudius had poisoned her first husband; and Hamlet dies, his mission at last accomplished. Those critics who regard Hamlet as the supreme egotist assume that he could kill the King only to avenge himself; but this ignores the development of his character in the last act of the play. Others have supposed that Hamlet was unable to act while his mother was alive, either because he and his uncle were rivals for her love, or because he could not justify his killing of the King without exposing her. Apart from the fact that such interpretations read between the lines in a dubious way,[1] they also ignore the change in Hamlet's character after his voyage.

The dying Hamlet—'noble Hamlet', as Laertes now admits—exchanges forgiveness with his penitent murderer; and, realising that his time is short, he begs Horatio to explain his cause to the unsatisfied. He does not wish to be regarded 'in the general censure' as a madman or a king-killer. Horatio, in accordance with his stoical views, wishes to commit suicide; but Hamlet makes him see that his love can be better expressed by continuing to live and ensuring that his friend does not have 'a wounded name':

[1] Ernest Jones, in his very ingenious *Hamlet and Œdipus*, attributes Hamlet's vacillation to 'the repression of infantile Œdipus wishes', which 'arouses unconscious resistances against the thought of killing his step-father' and to his inability 'to take action against the man whose crime coincides with his own unconscious wishes'. It is not, I suppose, impossible for Shakespeare, by looking in his own heart, to have depicted a man suffering from a neurosis unknown to the psychology of his day; but we cannot pluck out the heart of Hamlet's mystery so easily.

> If thou didst ever hold me in thy heart,
> Absent thee from felicity awhile,
> And in this harsh world draw thy breath in pain,
> To tell my story.

Hamlet is no longer afraid of what dreams may come after death: now his mission is accomplished, death is felicity and rest. His last thoughts are for the welfare of Denmark, and he supports the candidature of Fortinbras who arrives just too late to hear his dying words. The arrival of the English ambassadors at the same moment—only twenty lines after the death of Claudius—shows how narrowly Hamlet had succeeded in his task: the interim had been short indeed.

Horatio's valediction magically reminds us of the qualities and potentialities of the dead Prince, which had been partially hidden by the tragic situation in which he found himself, and it holds out hope of another world which would compensate for the miseries of this:

> Now cracks a noble heart. Good night, sweet prince,
> And flights of angels sing thee to thy rest!

Horatio then turns to Fortinbras to speak of the 'woe or wonder' of the spectacle. Shakespeare may have been thinking of the 'admiration and commiseration' which Sidney thought it was the function of tragedy to arouse. Horatio goes on to order, with the authority he derives from the dead Prince, that the bodies should be placed on a stage, so that in his funeral oration he can carry out his unspoken promise to report Hamlet and his cause. He would speak

> Of carnal, bloody, and unnatural acts; (*Claudius' murder of his brother, and his adultery*)
> Of accidental judgments, casual slaughters; (*The deaths of Polonius and Gertrude*)
> Of deaths put on by cunning and forc'd cause; (*The killing of Rosencrantz and Guildenstern*)
> And, in this upshot, purposes mistook
> Fall'n on th' inventors' heads. (*The deaths of Claudius and Laertes*)

The last word is with Fortinbras; and, although he does not yet know the true story, he reminds the audience that Hamlet the Dane was a warrior, that his long struggle with his mighty opposite had ended in victory, although that victory had cost him his life.

3. The Heart of the Mystery

In the course of this commentary on the action of the play we have had occasion to point out that a number of incidents have been interpreted in different ways: all Hamlet's main speeches, indeed, have been read in the light of a general theory of his character. 'Historical' critics have argued that such divergent interpretations are possible because Shakespeare was rewriting an old play, traces of the comparatively crude original remaining in the finished play, to such an extent that T. S. Eliot once regarded it as 'an artistic failure'. The Hamlet of 'To be or not to be', 'What a piece of work is a man!' or 'Alas! Poor Yorick!' is difficult to reconcile with the Hamlet who calls the Ghost 'this fellow in the cellarage', who insults Ophelia with his obscenities, who wishes to ensure the damnation as well as the death of his enemy, who murders Rosencrantz and Guildenstern without compunction, and who speaks of the corpse of his earlier victim as 'the guts'. So we have Waldock explaining the difficulties in *Hamlet* by saying that

> An old play is wrenched to new significances, significances, in places, that to the end it refuses to take. It was, perhaps, inevitable that the play should show signs, in fissures and strain, of all this forceful bending.

Santayana makes a similar point when he says that Shakespeare

> allowed the plot to suggest the characters, and conceived their motives and psychological movement only as an underpinning and satiric deepening for their known actions.

He goes on to suggest that some of Hamlet's actions and speeches

> apparently remain over from the old melodrama, and mark the points neglected by the poet and left untransmuted by his intuition. These survivals of cruder methods, if survivals they be, give a touch of positive incoherence to Hamlet's character, otherwise sufficiently complex.

It is possible, indeed, that Shakespeare revised the play more than once. There are a number of points which can be used to support this view. Hamlet's age at the beginning of the play appears to be about eighteen, and although Diane de Poitiers maintained her hold over Henri II until she was sixty, and Elizabeth I was officially admired after she had reached that age, one would not suppose Gertrude to be much more than forty; and yet, if we are to believe the First Grave-digger, Hamlet at the end of the play was thirty years old. Perhaps Shakespeare made the change either because he had endowed his hero with mature thoughts and feelings or because Burbage had become too old to pass as a very young man. Then again, Horatio seems at one moment to be a stranger to Denmark, and at another to know more about the causes of the armaments race than Bernardo or Marcellus. A third point is that the order of the scenes differs in the First Quarto—'To be or not to be' and the scene with Ophelia being put before the scene with Rosencrantz and Guildenstern—and Polonius and Reynaldo are called Corambis and Montano. Fourthly, some of the verse has been thought to be less mature than that of most of the play; and it is supposed that in the final revision Shakespeare left some of the early verse to stand unaltered, just as he left unfortunate traces of the earlier Hamlet in his sophisticated hero.

Yet the careless workmanship which this theory of imperfect revision implies seems hardly to square with the mere length of the play. Would Shakespeare, for the first time in his career, have written passages which he must have known would be cut in performance—written them, one supposes, for his own artistic satisfaction—if at the same time he was leaving in the text passages and incidents which were manifestly out of harmony with his final conception of the play? It is not, of course, impossible. His audience, familiar with the earlier Hamlet, might resent the omission of time-hallowed incidents; and, what is more important, Shakespeare himself, having been familiar with the play for more than a decade, may not have been fully aware of the incompatibilities which have worried some of his readers. But we ought not to fall back on the theory of imperfect revision without first seeing whether the difficulties may not have some other explanation, and whether they are as blatant and damaging as is sometimes pretended.

As for Hamlet's age, we cannot assume he was not more than eighteen because he was studying at the university or because he would otherwise have succeeded to the throne on the death of his father; nor, on the other hand, that he was actually thirty because the Gravedigger says so. Horatio in the first scene is a convenient vehicle for the provision of necessary information, but we cannot deduce anything about his character from the nature of this information. The order of scenes and the naming of characters in the First Quarto may be due to the influence not of an earlier version of Shakespeare's play but to that of the source-play. And, with regard to the verse, it could easily be shown that incidents which display the 'primitive' Hamlet (e.g. 'Now might I do it pat', remarks on the death of Polonius, the account of the forged death-warrant) are written in a more mature style, to judge by metrical characteristics, than some other parts of the play: there may well be purely dramatic reasons for differences in the verse.

If, then, we may assume that the script of *Hamlet*, which went to the printers of the Second Quarto, represents Shakespeare's considered intentions—but, it must be remembered, a dramatic script written for performance, and not for reading or close analysis—how is it, as we saw earlier, that the critics, at least during the last 200 years, have had diametrically opposed views on the meaning of the play and on the character of the hero? We can find support for almost any opinion we like to hold: that Hamlet ought not to have avenged his father's death, that he was a scoundrel worse even than Claudius, that he was a noble and heroic figure combining (as Peter Alexander says) sensitiveness and toughness, that he was in love with his mother or with Horatio, that he was mad, or that he did not even pretend to be mad. One is driven to sympathise with Oscar Wilde's question: 'Are Hamlet's critics mad, or only pretending to be so?'

It would not be difficult to show that most critics of the play make the mistake of selecting only those points which support their theories, ignoring passages of equal importance which do not; others read the play almost as if it were a novel, ignoring the temporal sequence of events, which is always of vital importance in dramatic literature, and reading between the lines; others, again, look at the play through modern spectacles, ignoring the conventions of the Elizabethan stage with regard to the presentation of character and, more seriously, crediting the author with an outlook he can scarcely have possessed; and, finally, there are those who go to the other extreme and assume that Shakespeare was utterly circumscribed by the commonplaces of his age. Madariaga, for example, and to a lesser extent, Rebecca West, tend to ignore the more favourable qualities of Hamlet's character; and Peter Alexander, perhaps, tends to ignore his defects. Strindberg spoke of Hamlet as a democrat and Landauer even pretended that he represented a prophetic vision of the classless society. On the other hand, there are critics who speak as though Shakespeare were compelled by the nature of the revenge play to treat the subject in the way he did. But, as we have seen, Chapman wrote a very different kind of revenge play; in *The Atheist's Tragedy* the Ghost orders his son to leave vengeance to heaven; in *The Malcontent* the villain is spared by the hero; in *The Spanish Tragedy* revenge is approved; and in *The Revenger's Tragedy* the avenger is more corrupted than Hamlet by his task. Professor John Lawlor, in a very ingenious essay, has shown that dramatists who made an explicit conflict between the duty of revenge and the demands of justice 'insensibly destroyed the thematic unity of the Revenge kind', substituting a kind of thesis play; and he suggests that Shakespeare deliberately prevented Hamlet from discussing whether it was right to avenge his father's death, although the Elizabethan audience would realise that Hamlet's delay was caused by 'a scruple about the justice of Revenge'.

Professor Lawlor, I think, here comes very close to the truth. Hamlet, indeed, does mention in his last soliloquy 'some craven scruple'; but I do not think that the audience is meant to doubt that Hamlet ought to avenge his father's death, that he ought to kill Claudius, that he ought to set right the disjointed time by getting rid of the usurper, even though it was proper for him to have scruples and doubts, and even though he was led to commit several wrong actions in pursuit of a right end. Hamlet's tragedy is a particular example of a universal predicament: action is necessary, but all action in a fallen world involves us in evil. To attempt to shuffle off responsibility by refusing to act, or by shuffling off this mortal coil—by 'handing God back his ticket', as Dostoevsky puts it—involves us equally in guilt.

Hamlet is a character of extraordinary complexity, and we should recognise that no simple formula will serve to pluck out the heart of his mystery. The noble mind to which Ophelia refers and the noble heart which cracks in the final scene, are overclouded throughout the play. There is no doubt that Shakespeare was aware of the characteristics of the melancholy man as outlined by Elizabethan psychologists, and that he made use of them in portraying his hero. When the Ghost enjoins Hamlet not to taint his mind, the injunction comes too late, for his mind is already tainted by his mother's hasty re-marriage and by the death of a father to whom he was devotedly attached. When he hears that his mother had been unfaithful before his father's death, that his father had not been stung by a serpent but murdered, and that he was suffering in purgatory for the 'foul crimes' he had committed in his lifetime, Hamlet's melancholy is intensified; and while he is still staggering under these successive blows the conduct of Ophelia seems to confirm his generalisation about the frailty of women. He feels what Wordsworth and Keats called 'the burden of the mystery', and he knows not 'the balance of good and evil'.

Realising that his possession of Claudius's guilty secret makes it impossible for him to behave normally, he puts on an antic disposition; but, instead of persuading the King that he is harmless, this ruse makes him an object of suspicion, and he is so closely watched that his task becomes more difficult to accomplish. He becomes inextricably tangled in a web of guilt. He uses Ophelia to persuade the King that rejected love has driven him into madness, as Polonius was later to use her to find its cause. In his antic disposition he becomes at times perilously close to the part he is playing; and it is often difficult to know whether we should take his speeches as expressions of his real feelings or of his *persona*. As Polonius sees, there is method in his madness. He can, like a bitter Fool—almost like the Fool in *King Lear* —inveigh against the stupidities and vices of humanity and indulge in obscenities which give an outlet to his real feelings of horror and disgust; and his treatment of Ophelia, explicable by his belief that he has been betrayed, exhibits the cruelty of a corrupted idealist.

When Hamlet listens to the story of his father's murder he has no doubt of its truth because it confirms the premonition of his prophetic soul. He assures Horatio that it is an honest ghost; but he cannot

sweep to his revenge, as he had promised to do, because he must first
have confirmation of the story. One cannot kill a man on the word of
a ghost, especially if one's enemy is a king, protected by Divine
Right, and especially if one stands to gain a crown by the deed.
Hamlet has to convince others, lest they should think that he, rather
than his uncle, had murdered to gain a crown. It is obvious from
several remarks by Rosencrantz and Guildenstern that they suspect
that the Prince's melancholy is caused by his feeling that he has been
cheated of the crown. Hamlet, moreover, is scrupulous enough to
know that however much he may be convinced of the contrary, the
spirit may have been a devil,

> yea, and perhaps
> Out of my weakness and my melancholy,
> As he is very potent with such spirits,
> Abuses me to damn me.

This fear was a real one, as Dover Wilson and others have shown, and
not merely an excuse for inaction. As Hamlet tells Horatio, if the
guilt of Claudius is not manifest during the performance of 'The
Murder of Gonzago',

> It is a damned ghost that we have seen,
> And my imaginations are as foul
> As Vulcan's stithy.

The very fact that he had had a premonition of Claudius's guilt before
his interview with the Ghost made it possible for him to believe in the
possibility that the Devil was using a delusion to trap him into
damnation.

The King's behaviour during the performance convinces both
Hamlet and his sceptical friend of the truth of the Ghost's story; but
the rest of the court have noticed nothing except the Prince's bad
taste in choosing such a play and his intolerable behaviour during its
performance. Still, after a lapse of months, Hamlet has obtained the
necessary confirmation, although, as we have seen, at the expense of
letting Claudius into his secret. Just after he has proclaimed that he is
ready to drink hot blood, he is provided immediately with an opportunity of killing the King. He lets it go by because he is unable to

strike a defenceless man—one who seems almost to have taken sanctuary—and he rationalises his reluctance by saying that such an act would ensure his enemy's salvation. This, I think, is the only point where our interpretation necessitates reading between the lines; but such an interpretation of this episode appears to be demanded, as we have seen, by Hamlet's opening words: 'Now might I do it.' The alternative is to assume, as some critics have done, that Hamlet gives us the real reason for his reluctance; and this would be difficult, though not absolutely impossible, to reconcile with Hamlet's other actions and speeches. His desire to damn as well as to kill Claudius would then spring from his remembrance of his father's present sufferings. Yet the rage against the King into which Hamlet works himself parallels the impotent rage he displays after the Hecuba speech; and, in any case, as G. R. Elliott has shown, it is Hamlet's personal hatred of Claudius that, throughout the play, contaminates his desire for justice. This is made apparent, too, in the violence of his speeches to his mother in the following scene. Although he does make Gertrude repent, it is difficult not to agree with L. C. Knights when he says that Hamlet is 'fascinated by what he condemns'. His attitude to sexual love is manifestly warped, and although one can explain this by the shock of his mother's adultery, one cannot wholly excuse it. His attitude to the killing of Polonius oscillates between callousness and repentance, and in his last words before he leaves for England he exclaims:

> O! from this time forth,
> My thoughts be bloody or be nothing worth.

But, as we have seen, Hamlet's *thoughts* have been bloodthirsty enough; and if Claudius, instead of the father of the woman he loved, had been hiding behind the arras, his task would have been accomplished and the play would have been over. As the only real opportunity for killing Claudius was when he found him at his prayers, we are driven to assume that it was what he calls 'some craven scruple' which stayed his hand, rather than the desire to have a more complete and fiendish revenge.

Hamlet returns from his voyage, quieter and more confident; and the change appears to be due to his belief that providence has given

him a sign that an opportunity will be provided, and that it is therefore unnecessary to seek out the means of executing justice on the
King. To L. C. Knights 'The readiness is all' is merely 'the paradoxical
recognition of a truth glimpsed in defeat': it seems rather to express
Hamlet's new trust in providence, and to be a prelude to his triumph
rather than to his defeat.

It is, of course, true that during the course of the play Hamlet, by
his ill luck, his errors of judgment, and by his involvement in evil,
has been the cause of misery to others. If he had been as single-minded
and ruthless as Pyrrhus, Fortinbras, and Laertes, he might have accomplished his revenge without the trail of deaths which he left
behind. But in spite of these tragic results of what Abercrombie
called 'the heroism of moral vacillation', it is obvious that to allow
reason to fust in us unused and to act without due consideration puts
us on the level of the beasts, while if we look before and after and
weigh the consequences of our actions, we find it more and more
difficult to act at all. Hamlet cannot rely on the conventional code of
the rotten society in which he lives, nor accept without thinking the
crude imperatives of the revenger's ethic. He is wrung by the anguish
of choice, because he knows that on him depends the fate of the king-
dom to which he is the rightful heir. Rebecca West perversely credits
Hamlet, 'this bad man', with a single good action, when he uses his
last moments to choose his successor to the throne. She is right,
although she exaggerates, to stress Hamlet's involvement in evil, and
the evil that he himself does and thinks; but she surely underestimates
his nobler qualities and the sheer difficulty of the situation in which he
finds himself, and she ignores the development of his character in the
last act of the play.

What, indeed, could Hamlet have done? He could, of course, have
repudiated his mission, as L. C. Knights would have wished, on the
grounds that the Ghost's demands were evil and unchristian. This
might have made an interesting play—the kind of play Shakespeare
was to write in his final period—but it was obviously not the kind of
play which the Hamlet story demanded of a dramatist. The hero was
bound to accept the killing of Claudius as a duty; and can one
honestly say that he should have left the murderer to enjoy the fruits
of his crime? A different Hamlet, one like the Amleth of Saxo

Grammaticus's story, might have killed his uncle on the strength of the Ghost's accusation, ascended the throne, married Ophelia, and lived happily ever after. But such a primitive hero was not likely to be of interest to Shakespeare when he was at the height of his creative powers. What he did was to imagine a 'noble' and 'sweet' Prince, sensitive, sophisticated, and intelligent, placed in a situation where his acknowledged duty could only be repugnant—as it would be repugnant to Hamlet's critics if they·were unfortunate enough to find themselves in his position—and where his intelligence made his duty all the more difficult. To this extent Coleridge was right. Naturally enough, Hamlet's sense of frustration combines with the initial shock to his youthful idealism, and his repression is relieved only in outbursts of violence and verbal cruelty. It would be wrong to romanticise or sentimentalise his character; but his faults may be regarded as the occupational disease of avengers.

When all is said, Hamlet is neither a novel nor a psychological case-book, but a play; and in the theatre the problems which have baffled the critics do not arise. An audience may argue about the play, but it never doubts the reality of the hero. The very fact that he is not so easily played upon as a pipe adds to our belief in his reality. It was never Shakespeare's method to create characters who could be neatly pigeon-holed. Writing scripts for performance, he allows some licence of interpretation to the actor, and leaves the audience with a wholesome sense of the mystery of human personality.

A Short Bibliography

(The following list omits the great critics of the past)

A. J. A. Waldock, 'Hamlet': A Study in Critical Method (1931)

J. D. Wilson, What Happens in 'Hamlet' (1935)

H. Granville-Barker, Preface to 'Hamlet' (1936)

L. L. Schücking, The Meaning of 'Hamlet' (1937)

J. E. Hankins, The Character of Hamlet (1941)

G. I. Duthie, The 'Bad' Quarto of Hamlet (1941)

C. S. Lewis, Hamlet—the Prince or the Poem (1943)

R. Walker, The Time is Out of Joint (1948)

E. Jones, Hamlet and Œdipus (1949)

A. A. Jack, Young Hamlet (1950)

G. R. Elliott, Scourge and Minister (1951)

B. L. Joseph, Conscience and the King (1953)

P. Alexander, Hamlet, Father and Son (1955)

H. Levin, The Question of 'Hamlet' (1959)

L. C. Knights, An Approach to 'Hamlet' (1960)

J. R. Brown and B. Harris, Hamlet (1963)

M. Holmes, The Guns of Elsinore (1964)

M. Weitz, Hamlet and the Philosophy of Literary Criticism (1965)

E. Prosser, Hamlet and Revenge (1967)

M. Charney, Style in Hamlet (1969)

N. Alexander, Poison, Play and Duel (1971)

H. Fisch, Hamlet and the Word (1971)

G. W. Knight, The Wheel of Fire (1930, 1949)

L. B. Campbell, Shakespeare's Tragic Heroes (1930)

E. E. Stoll, Art and Artifice in Shakespeare (1935)

C. F. E. Spurgeon, Shakespeare's Imagery (1935)

F. Fergusson, The Idea of a Theater (1949)

W. H. Clemen, The Development of Shakespeare's Imagery (1951)

D. G. James, The Dream of Learning (1951)

H. D. F. Kitto, Form and Meaning in Drama (1956)

J. Lawlor, The Tragic Sense in Shakespeare (1960)

L. Kirschbaum, Character and Characterization in Shakespeare (1962)

V. K. Whitaker, The Mirror up to Nature (1965)